THE
TOTALLY
EGGPLANT
COOKBOOK

THE
TOTALLY
EGGPLANT
COOKBOOK

By Helene Siegel

Illustrated by
Carolyn Vibbert

CELESTIAL ARTS
BERKELEY, CALIFORNIA

Celestial Arts Publishing
P.O. Box 7123
Berkeley, CA 94707

Cover design and illustration: Bob Greisen
Interior design and typesetting: Susan Hernday
Interior illustrations: Carolyn Vibbert

The Totally Eggplant Cookbook is produced by becker&mayer!, Ltd.

Lyrics from "Eggplant" by Michael Franks © 1977 Mississippi Mud
Music Co. (BMI). Reprinted with permission.

Library of Congress Cataloging-in-Publication Data:
Siegel, Helene.
    Totally Eggplant Cookbook/ by Helene Siegel.
        p.   cm.
    ISBN 0-89087-787-4
    1. Cookery (Eggplant)   2. Eggplant   I. Title.
    TX803.E4S54 1996
    641.6'5646—dc20   95-139671   CIP

Other cookbooks in this series:

The Totally Picnic Cookbook
The Totally Pizza Cookbook
The Totally Tomato Cookbook

CONTENTS

INTRODUCTION

My lady sticks to me like white on rice
She never cooks the same way twice
Maybe it's the mushrooms, maybe the tomatoes.
Can't reveal her name, but eggplant is her game.
—from "Eggplant" by Michael Franks

During a steamy summer in Los Angeles, while nibbling on assorted salads at a sidewalk cafe in the kind of neighborhood where nobody (female) weighs more than 120 pounds, I came to an important realization. I realized that one of the most perfect summer foods is eggplant, or more precisely, grilled eggplant marinated with olive oil, fresh herbs, and garlic—the dish I was nibbling on at the moment.

What more could
a health-conscious yet
serious eater ask for? It's lighter
than meat, it absorbs flavors brilliantly, and it melts in your mouth
while sending pleasingly complex
messages to your brain.

Since those salad days, I have had the
continued pleasure of experimenting with
eggplant. And while grilling remains a
favorite way of cooking it, I have also discovered, like the lady in the song, that eggplant is
a vegetable of many possibilities. Grill it, fry it,
stuff it, roll it, bake it, or braise it. As the Turks
know, who have more than a hundred ways to
cook it, eggplant is a very versatile vegetable.
And it's economical, to boot!

My greatest eggplant moment, however,
came when I realized that frying could
more or less be eliminated in favor of
healthier and quicker roasting. Here is
how to do it: Simply lay slices on a

cookie sheet, sprinkle with oil and salt, and bake in a very hot (450–500 degrees F) oven. Voilà, cooking with eggplant is no longer a time consuming oily mess, but an every-day affair.

So if, like the lady in the song, you feel an affinity for the unctuous purple vegetable (that is really a fruit), just peruse the recipes contained herein and then start cooking. Who knows? Eggplant may become your game too.

When my baby cooks her eggplant
She don't read no book
She's got a giocónda *kind of dirty look.*
—Michael Franks

SAVORY SOUPS
AND
APPETIZERS

CURRIED EGGPLANT SOUP

Curry and eggplant are a terrific combination from the Indian kitchen.

2 medium eggplants
olive oil for coating
salt and freshly ground pepper
3 tablespoons olive oil
1 medium onion, sliced
4 garlic cloves, sliced
2 slices fresh ginger, peeled,
    crushed, and chopped
2 teaspoons curry powder
1/2 teaspoon sugar
2 cups chicken stock
2 cups water
2 tablespoons fresh chopped basil
    and 1/2 cup buttermilk as
    garnish (optional)

Preheat oven to 450 degrees F.

Remove stems, cut eggplants in half lengthwise, and score in a crisscross pattern. Rub with olive oil, sprinkle with salt and pepper. Bake, cutside up, 1 hour, until soft. When cool to touch, remove pulp and chop.

Heat oil in stockpot over medium heat. Cook onion, garlic, ginger, salt, and pepper until onions are soft and golden. Stir in curry powder and sugar, turn heat to high, and cook, stirring frequently, about 2 minutes longer. Pour in chicken stock, water, and eggplant. Bring to boil, reduce to simmer, and cook 10 minutes. Skim and discard foam.

Transfer to food processor and purée in batches until smooth. Return to pot to heat through, and season with basil and buttermilk.

SERVES 4 TO 6

ROASTED EGGPLANT AND POTATO SOUP

This soothing, smoky purée is perfect on cold winter nights.

1 large eggplant
3 tablespoons butter
1 medium onion, chopped
1 tablespoon minced garlic
1 1/2 teaspoons paprika
1/4 teaspoon cayenne
1/4 teaspoon ground cumin
salt
4 cups chicken stock
1 1/2 pounds boiling potatoes, unpeeled
    and chopped
1/2 cup plain yogurt for garnish (optional)

Preheat broiler and move the rack about 8 inches from the heat. Broil eggplant until charred all over, about 40 minutes. Let cool, peel, and roughly chop.

Melt butter in stockpot over medium heat. Sauté onion and garlic until soft. Stir in paprika, cayenne, cumin, salt, and eggplant. Turn up heat and stir for 1 minute. Pour in chicken stock and potatoes. Bring to boil, reduce to simmer, and cook until potatoes are done, 35 to 40 minutes. Purée in food processor and rewarm if necessary. Ladle into serving bowls and swirl in yogurt, if desired.

SERVES 4

Purchasing and Storage
Look for smooth, taut, shiny skin when purchasing eggplant; wrinkled and blemished eggplants should be avoided. A good eggplant should feel heavy in your hand, and should bounce right back when pressed with a thumb. Eggplants are best stored at room temperature, not in the refrigerator. They do not keep long; 2 or 3 days at most.

EGGPLANT CAVIAR

*Serve this robust roasted eggplant dip
with strong black olives,
crudités, and thin slices of baguette
for dipping.*

2 medium eggplants, trimmed
olive oil for coating
salt and freshly ground pepper
5 garlic cloves, peeled
2 tablespoons olive oil
3 tablespoons lemon juice
$1/2$ medium onion, chopped

Preheat oven to 450 degrees F. Cut eggplants in half lengthwise and score in
crisscross pattern. Rub all over with
olive oil, sprinkle with salt and pepper,
and bake, cut-side up, about 1 hour,
until soft. When cool enough to handle,
scrape out pulp and roughly chop.

With food processor on, add garlic to mince. Add eggplant, olive oil, and lemon juice, and purée until smooth. Season to taste with salt and pepper, and pulse to combine. Transfer to mixing bowl, stir in onions, and serve at room temperature or chilled.

SERVES 6

Eggplants by Size
Japanese eggplants are the long, thin, purple variety stocked in the supermarket. They never need to be salted or peeled. For the purposes of this book, eggplants under 1 pound are classified as small, 1 to 1 1/2 pounds is medium, and anything more than 1 1/2 pounds is large. The larger the eggplant, the more seeds and moisture. To trim an eggplant, simply slice off the green stem at the top.

SICILIAN CAPONATA

I love caponata, the traditional sweet and sour relish of southern Italy, for sprucing up grilled fish and chicken, or simply for spreading on crackers.

1 large eggplant, trimmed and cut
    into ¹/₂-inch cubes
olive oil
salt and freshly ground pepper
¹/₂ cup red wine vinegar
¹/₃ cup currants
2 tablespoons olive oil
1 onion, roughly chopped
2 celery ribs, trimmed and thinly
    sliced
¹/₂ cup large Italian *or* Greek green
    olives, in chunks
¹/₃ cup capers, drained
2 tablespoons sugar
¹/₄ cup tomato paste

Preheat oven to 450 degrees F. Arrange eggplant in single layer in roasting dish. Drizzle with oil, sprinkle with salt and pepper, and bake until it begins to brown, 40 minutes. Reserve.

Meanwhile combine red wine vinegar and currants in small bowl and set aside to plump.

In large skillet, heat oil over moderate heat. Cook onion and celery until soft but not brown. Add the vinegar and currants, olives, capers, sugar, and tomato paste. Stir well, reduce heat, and simmer about 8 minutes. Stir in eggplant and cook an additional 3 to 5 minutes. Serve at room temperature or slightly chilled.

SERVES 6

BABA GHANOUSH

Everybody's favorite eggplant dip is almost as easy to make as it is to buy. Serve with toasted pita triangles and veggies or as a sandwich spread as on page 72.

1 large eggplant
3 tablespoons tahini *or*
   sesame seed paste
1 tablespoon olive oil
1 tablespoon lemon juice
2 teaspoons minced garlic
¼ teaspoon paprika
4 dashes Tabasco
2 tablespoons eggplant liquid
salt and freshly ground pepper
   to taste

Preheat broiler. Broil eggplant, turning occasionally, until evenly charred and soft, about 40 minutes. Transfer to bowl to cool. When cool enough to handle, peel, reserving liquid in bowl. Roughly chop pulp and transfer to mixing bowl.

Add remaining ingredients, mixing and mashing to form a chunky dip. Adjust seasonings to taste and serve chilled or at room temperature.

MAKES 2 CUPS, 4 SERVINGS

Eggplant Taboos

Do anything you like with eggplant, but NEVER boil, blanch, or freeze it, and NEVER serve it raw. This is one fruit/vegetable that is always better fried, grilled, or roasted. It also has been known to turn nasty when cooked in aluminum.

PERSIAN EGGPLANT DIP

Smoky, sweet, and sour merge elegantly in this Iranian eggplant purée. Serve with radishes, celery sticks, and pita crisps.

2 medium eggplants
1½ tablespoons minced garlic
½ cup plain low fat yogurt
¼ teaspoon cinnamon
salt and freshly ground pepper
    to taste
2 tablespoons olive oil
1 medium onion,
    very thinly sliced
1 tablespoon chopped fresh
    mint for garnish

Preheat broiler. Broil eggplants, turning occasionally, until charred all over and soft. Set aside to cool. When cool enough to handle, peel and transfer pulp to bowl of food processor.

Add garlic, yogurt, and cinnamon. Pulse to make a rough purée. (Do not overprocess—it should remain chunky.) Transfer to mixing bowl and season to taste with salt and pepper.

Heat olive oil in small skillet over medium-low heat. Cook onion, stirring frequently, until soft and browned. Stir into eggplant mixture, adjust seasonings, garnish with mint, and serve chilled or at room temperature.

Makes 2 cups, 4 to 6 servings

GRILLED EGGPLANT
AND
SMOKED MOZZARELLA

olive oil for brushing
$^1/_4$ cup olive oil
2 tablespoons balsamic vinegar
2 teaspoons minced sun-dried
   tomatoes packed in oil
1 teaspoon minced garlic
salt and freshly ground pepper
1 medium eggplant, stemmed
   and cut in $^1/_4$-inch slices across
   width
6 ounces smoked mozzarella,
   sliced

Preheat grill or broiler and brush grate or tray with oil.

In small bowl, whisk together olive oil, vinegar, tomatoes, garlic, salt, and pepper.

Brush eggplant slices on both sides with olive oil and grill or broil until charred on one side, about 4 minutes. Turn, top each with a slice of cheese, and cook until cheese melts. (If grilling, cover grill to melt cheese.) Transfer to platter and drizzle with reserved dressing. Serve warm or at room temperature.

SERVES 4

Some people use coarse salt to draw out the egg-plant's sharpness, but why try and change the nature of a vegetable that has some personality?
    —*Chef Roger Vergé*

EGGPLANT ROLLS WITH GOAT CHEESE VINAIGRETTE

This typical Sicilian antipasto is an adaptation of a favorite from Valentino's restaurant, a Los Angeles landmark.

2 medium eggplants, trimmed and
    cut lengthwise into $^{1}/_{2}$-inch slices
olive oil
salt
8 ounces ($^{1}/_{2}$ cup) soft goat cheese
$^{1}/_{4}$ cup red wine vinegar
$^{1}/_{4}$ cup olive oil
1 teaspoon minced garlic
$^{1}/_{4}$ cup chopped fresh basil, Italian
    parsley, *or* mint
salt and freshly ground pepper

Preheat oven to 500 degrees F. Coat baking tray with olive oil. Arrange eggplant slices in single layer, drizzle tops with additional oil, season with salt, and bake about 6 minutes per side, until browned along edges. Let cool.

When cool enough to handle, spread a generous teaspoon of goat cheese across width and roll to enclose. Place rolls, seam-side down (do not worry about slits), in glass or ceramic dish.

In small bowl, whisk together vinegar, olive oil, garlic, herbs, salt, and pepper. Drizzle over eggplant rolls, cover with plastic wrap, and chill at least 4 hours or up to 4 days.

SERVES 6 TO 8

EGGPLANT CROSTINI WITH POACHED EGGS

Here is a nice low calorie alternative to eggs Benedict for a special breakfast.

olive oil
1 Japanese eggplant, cut diagonally into $1/2$-inch slices
4 ($3/4$-inch) slices Italian *or* French bread
4 slices Gruyère *or* Swiss cheese
1 tablespoon chopped fresh basil, chives, *or* parsley
salt and freshly ground pepper
4 eggs, poached and kept warm

Preheat broiler and place
rack about 8 inches from heat.

Lightly coat baking tray with
olive oil. Arrange eggplant slices
on one side and bread on another.
Drizzle tops with olive oil. Broil eggplant until golden on both sides, and
reserve. Broil bread until golden on one
side. Remove from oven, turn bread, top
each slice with cheese, and return to oven
to melt.

Place each bread slice on serving plate.
Top with eggplant slices to cover and one
poached egg. Sprinkle with herbs, salt, and
pepper, and serve.

SERVES 4

EGGPLANT FRITTERS

The contrast between the jelly-like interior and crisp coating in these fried disks is irresistible. Serve quickly for best texture.

1 cup all-purpose flour
$1/2$ teaspoon baking powder
1 teaspoon salt
1 teaspoon black pepper
$1/2$ teaspoon sugar
1 teaspoon dried crumbled
   oregano
$1^1/2$ cups warm beer
6 cups vegetable oil
1 medium eggplant, peeled and
   cut crosswise into $3/8$-inch slices
salt for sprinkling
plain yogurt for dipping

Combine flour, baking powder, salt, pepper, sugar, and oregano in mixing bowl. Pour in beer, whisk until smooth, and let sit at room temperature for 1 hour.

Heat oil in large pot or fryer to 350 degrees F. Dip each eggplant slice into batter to evenly coat, shake off excess, and drop into hot oil, being careful not to crowd the pan. Fry until golden brown all over, 3 to 5 minutes. Use slotted spoon to turn, and transfer to paper towels to drain. Serve hot, sprinkled with salt, and with yogurt for dipping.

SERVES 4

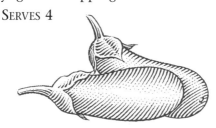

ASIAN EGGPLANT SKEWERS

Eggplant and mushrooms are great absorbers of other flavors. Serve over mixed salad greens as a starter, or chill and serve as a cold accompaniment to grilled beef.

8 Japanese eggplants, trimmed
3 portobello *or* 32 white
    mushroom caps, wiped clean
$1/2$ cup peanut oil
$1/2$ cup rice wine vinegar
$1/4$ cup soy sauce
1 tablespoon grated fresh ginger
1 tablespoon minced garlic
$1/4$ teaspoon red chile flakes

Preheat broiler. Lightly coat eggplants with oil, and broil, turning once, until slightly softened. Let cool and cut into 1-inch lengths. If using portobello caps, cut into 2-inch chunks. (Leave white caps whole.)

Whisk together peanut oil, rice wine vinegar, soy sauce, ginger, garlic, and chile flakes in shallow roasting dish or casserole. Thread 8 skewers with alternating eggplant chunks and mushroom caps. Place in dish to marinate one hour at room temperature, turning occasionally to marinate evenly.

Reheat broiler. Arrange skewers on broiler tray or grill, and cook about 6 minutes, turning frequently, until lightly charred all over. Serve hot or cold.

SERVES 4

Eggplant in the New World
How exactly the eggplant entered the New World is unclear, but a few theories have developed. One such theory proposes that African slaves brought it along with okra, watermelon, and black-eyed peas. Another suggests eggplant migrated from the Caribbean, Louisiana, or Mexico. The first American cookbook in which eggplant appeared was The Carolina Housewife, *published in 1847 by Sarah Routledge, who called it guinea squash, possibly for the African region from which it may have come.*

EGGPLANT FRONT AND CENTER

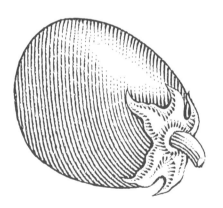

BAKED PENNE AND EGGPLANT CASSEROLE

Macaroni and cheese—with eggplant. What a good way to sneak some vegetables into a kid's diet!

1 pound penne *or* small tube pasta
olive oil
1 large eggplant, unpeeled, cut
    in 2 x ½ x ½-inch strips
2 cups shredded mozzarella cheese
¾ cup grated Parmesan
salt and pepper to taste
3 medium tomatoes, sliced across
    width
6 basil leaves

Cook pasta, drain, rinse with cold water, drain, and return to cooking pot. Toss with tablespoon or two of olive oil and set aside. Lightly coat a

9 x 13-inch ovenproof casserole with oil and set aside.

Pour oil into large skillet to a depth of $\frac{1}{2}$ inch. Over high heat, cook eggplant in single layer, in batches, until golden brown, stirring frequently with slotted spoon. Drain on paper towels.

Add eggplant to pasta and gently toss to combine without breaking. Add mozzarella, $\frac{1}{2}$ cup Parmesan, salt, and pepper, and mix.

Preheat oven to 350 degrees F.

Arrange the tomatoes in single layer in pre-pared casserole. Sprinkle with basil. Spoon on the pasta mixture and smooth top. Sprinkle with remaining $\frac{1}{4}$ cup Parmesan. Cover with aluminum foil and bake 20 minutes. Remove foil, turn heat to 425 degrees F, and bake 5 to 10 minutes, until top is golden and crusty. Serve hot.

SERVES 4 TO 6

PROVENÇAL VEGETABLE GRATIN

These vegetables and herbs are so vibrant that I serve this with only a loaf of crusty olive bread to highlight its simplicity. The recipe is inspired by the French chef Roger Vergé.

3 tablespoons plus $\frac{1}{2}$ cup olive oil
2 large onions, thinly sliced
3 red bell peppers, cored, seeded, and thinly sliced
2 medium eggplants, trimmed, peeled, and thinly sliced diagonally
3 medium zucchinis, trimmed, and thinly sliced diagonally
3 medium tomatoes, thinly sliced
6 garlic cloves, minced
2 tablespoons chopped fresh basil
$\frac{1}{2}$ teaspoon coarse salt and freshly ground pepper

Heat 3 tablespoons oil in large skillet over moderate heat. Cook onions until soft. Add peppers, reduce heat to low, and cook until vegetables are limp, about 20 minutes longer.

Preheat oven to 400 degrees F.

Coat the bottom of 9 x 13-inch ovenproof casserole with three-quarters of the onion mixture. Cover with a layer of half the eggplant slices, followed by half the zucchini and the remaining onion mixture. Top with a layer of eggplant, followed by zucchini, and then top with tomato slices.

In small bowl, mix together remaining olive oil, garlic, basil, salt, and pepper. Drizzle over top. Bake for 1 hour. Let sit 5 minutes, pour off excess oil, cut in squares, and serve hot or at room temperature. Leftovers make great sandwiches.

SERVES 6

FUSILLI WITH GRILLED EGGPLANT AND FRESH TOMATOES

Simplicity itself—a handful of basil, some chopped tomatoes, and grilled eggplant. A great low calorie, economical dish for the frazzled summer cook.

3 large Japanese eggplants, stemmed and thinly sliced lengthwise
olive oil for brushing
salt
$1/4$ cup olive oil
3 garlic cloves, roughly chopped
2 large ripe tomatoes, seeded and chopped
freshly ground pepper
1 pound fusilli *or* other corkscrew pasta, cooked and drained
3 tablespoons chopped fresh basil
grated Parmesan cheese

Preheat broiler and adjust rack 4 inches from flame. Lightly coat baking tray with olive oil and arrange eggplant in single layer. Sprinkle with salt, drizzle tops with oil, and broil until lightly charred, about 5 minutes per side. Cool and cut into $1/4$-inch diagonal strips, across width.

In small saucepan over high heat, cook olive oil with garlic until aroma is released. Add tomatoes, salt, and pepper. Reduce to simmer, and cook until tomatoes release their liquid, about 10 minutes.

Toss pasta with tomato mixture. Add eggplant, basil, and a few handfuls of Parmesan and toss well. Serve with additional Parmesan.

Serves 2 to 4

ROASTED EGGPLANT AND RED PEPPER PIZZA

Who can resist charred eggplant and pepper on a crusty, garlic pizza?

1 Japanese eggplant, unpeeled and cut in $1/4$-inch rounds
olive oil
salt
1 large prepared pizza crust
$1\frac{1}{2}$ cups grated mozzarella cheese
5 tablespoons soft goat cheese
$1/2$ teaspoon minced garlic
$1/2$ red bell pepper, roasted, peeled, and cut in strips
3 fresh basil leaves, chopped

Preheat oven to 500 degrees F. Coat a baking tray with olive oil and place eggplant rounds in single layer. Drizzle tops with olive oil, season with salt, and bake 3 to 4 minutes per side, until golden brown all over. (Use tongs to turn delicate slices.) Remove from pan and set aside to cool. Reduce heat to 450 degrees F.

Place pizza crust on same baking tray. Scatter mozzarella cheese, leaving crust bare along edges. Dot with 2 tablespoons of the goat cheese. Sprinkle with garlic and arrange eggplant in spoke pattern. Top with strips of pepper, basil, and the remaining crumbled goat cheese. Bake about 10 minutes, until cheese melts. Cut into wedges and serve hot.

SERVES 2

GRILLED SWORDFISH WITH EGGPLANT SALSA

Zesty eggplant salsa also goes well with grilled chicken.

3 tablespoons olive oil
1 medium eggplant, unpeeled and diced
salt
1 plum tomato, seeded and diced
2 tablespoons capers
1 teaspoon minced garlic
grated zest of 1 lemon
2 tablespoons chopped fresh Italian parsley
freshly ground pepper
4 (4-ounce) swordfish fillets

Heat olive oil in a
large skillet over high heat.
Sauté eggplant with salt, until
golden and soft but still holding
a shape, about 6 minutes. Set
aside to cool.

Combine tomato, capers, garlic,
lemon zest, and parsley in mixing
bowl. Add eggplant and toss gently.
Season to taste with salt and pepper, and
set aside at room temperature.

Season swordfish all over with salt and
pepper. Preheat grill and coat grate with oil.
Cook swordfish about 5 minutes per side, or
pan-fry in a thin layer of oil over high heat.
Transfer fish to serving plates, spoon on salsa,
and serve.

SERVES 4, MAKES 2 CUPS SALSA

IMAM BAYILDI

A legend about this traditional Turkish meal tells us that the imam, or priest, fainted with joy when his wife served him this luscious dish of onions and eggplant.

8 Japanese eggplants
$3/4$ cup olive oil
2 large onions, thinly sliced
3 tomatoes, (2 seeded and chopped, 1 sliced)
4 garlic cloves, minced
1 bunch Italian parsley, chopped
salt and fresh ground pepper

Preheat oven to 350 degrees F.
With stems intact, make stripes by peeling narrow lengthwise strips of eggplant skin about 1 inch apart. Heat oil in very large skillet over high heat.

Cook eggplants until golden all over. Set aside to drain and cool on paper towels.

Drain all but 2 tablespoons of oil from pan, reduce heat to medium, and cook onions, stirring frequently, until soft. Add chopped tomatoes, garlic, parsley, salt, and pepper, and continue cooking until onions just begin to caramelize, about 5 minutes longer. Cool.

Spread a thin layer of onion mixture on bottom of 9 x 13-inch casserole. Arrange eggplants on top in single layer and cut a lengthwise slit in each. Spoon onion mixture into each to stuff, and top each with a tomato slice. Season with salt and pepper. Bake 40 minutes, until bottom of pan is nearly dry. Cool and serve.

Serves 4

STUFFED EGGPLANT SICILIAN STYLE

The idea for this rich meat dish came from Michael Villella, whose mother cooked a similar specialty on feast days when he was growing up in Detroit.

4 large eggplants, trimmed and
    quartered
1 cup dry Italian bread, crust removed
    and cubed
1/2 pound ground beef
1 egg, beaten
1/2 cup grated Romano *or* Parmesan
    cheese
1 teaspoon minced garlic
2 teaspoons dried crumbled oregano
freshly ground pepper
1/4 cup olive oil
2 1/2 cups tomato sauce

Lightly score eggplant, and steam until soft, about 20 minutes. Set aside.

Soak bread cubes in water and squeeze out excess. Combine in bowl with beef, egg, $1/4$ cup of the cheese, garlic, oregano, and pepper. When cool, remove eggplant pulp, leaving $1/2$-inch shell intact, and chop. Combine pulp with meat mixture and divide into 8 portions. Stuff each shell.

Preheat oven to 350 degrees F.

Heat half the olive oil in skillet over high heat. Brown each shell on stuffing side and set aside, stuffing-side up. (Use remaining 2 tablespoons oil for frying.)

Coat bottom of 9 x 13-inch baking pan with a cup of tomato sauce. Arrange shells, stuffing-side up, in sauce. Spoon remaining sauce over top, and bake, uncovered, 1 hour, basting occasionally. Sprinkle top with remaining cheese and serve hot with pasta.

SERVES 4

SLIPPERY EGGPLANT AND PORK

The trick to successful stir-frying is to have all the ingredients nearby and ready to go into the pan in a flash. This is a great economical dish to serve over white rice.

¼ cup chicken stock
2 tablespoons hoisin sauce
1 tablespoon dry sherry
½ teaspoon sesame oil
¼ teaspoon Chinese chile sauce
2 tablespoons peanut *or* vegetable oil
½ pound ground pork
1 tablespoon minced garlic
1 tablespoon minced fresh ginger
3 Japanese eggplants, stemmed and thinly sliced diagonally
¼ cup fresh cilantro leaves

Mix together chicken stock, hoisin sauce, sherry, sesame oil, and chile sauce. Set aside.

Heat wok or large skillet over high heat. Add 1 tablespoon peanut oil and pork.

Stir-fry until no longer pink, and transfer to platter with slotted spoon. Drain liquid from pan and add remaining tablespoon peanut oil. Return wok to high heat.

Add garlic and ginger and stir-fry briefly, then add eggplant slices and stir-fry until evenly coated with oil, 1 minute. Pour in sauce mixture, stir to combine, and return pork to pan. Stir-fry 2 minutes longer, reduce heat, cover pan, and simmer about 1 minute. Turn out onto platter, sprinkle with cilantro, and serve hot.

SERVES 2 TO 4

POLENTA EGGPLANT LASAGNE

Kerry Hannawell of Silver Lake, California came up with this delicious vegetarian entrée. Make polenta ahead.

TOMATO SAUCE

2 tablespoons olive oil
1/2 small onion, chopped
2 garlic cloves, minced
1 (28-ounce) can crushed tomatoes
1 teaspoon dried sage
salt and freshly ground pepper

LASAGNE

$1/2$ (13.2-ounce) package (about 1 cup) instant polenta
2 medium eggplants, peeled and cut crosswise into $1/2$-inch slices
olive oil for sprinkling
2 cups grated smoked mozzarella
$1/4$ cup grated Parmesan cheese

Heat oil in skillet over moderate heat. Cook onion and garlic until soft. Stir in tomatoes, sage, salt, and pepper, and bring to boil. Reduce to simmer, and cook about 15 minutes.

Follow polenta package directions. Pour polenta into coated 8 x 12-inch glass or ceramic casserole, smooth top, and cool. Cover with plastic and chill overnight.

Preheat oven to 450 degrees F. Arrange eggplant slices on oil-coated baking sheets. Sprinkle with oil and salt. Bake until golden on both sides, about 10 minutes per side.

Invert polenta to remove. Line bottom of polenta pan with half eggplant slices. Top with half the tomato sauce and polenta. Cover with mozzarella, remaining tomato sauce, and eggplant. Sprinkle on Parmesan and bake until heated through, about 30 minutes. Cool slightly and serve.

SERVES 6 TO 8

SAUSAGE SKEWERS WITH EGGPLANT AND MUSHROOMS

Serve these sweet and spicy skewers with honey mustard for dipping.

$1/2$ cup plus 2 tablespoons olive oil

2 tablespoons minced garlic

$1/4$ teaspoon red chile flakes

3 Japanese eggplants, unpeeled and cut into $1/2$-inch slices

6 ounces shiitake mushroom caps, cleaned

4 smoky sweet sausages such as chicken and apple or turkey

In Egypt when a person rolls his eyes and says, "Here comes eggplant season," it's not time to heat up the grill. He's calling you crazy.

Whisk together ½ cup olive oil, garlic, and chile flakes in shallow bowl. Add eggplant and mushrooms, toss to coat, and marinate 30 minutes to 1 hour.

Preheat grill or broiler.

Heat remaining oil in skillet and sauté sausages until lightly and evenly browned. Drain on paper towels and cut into 1-inch slices. Thread 8 skewers with alternating sausage, mushrooms, and eggplant, and broil or grill over moderate flame, turning frequently until evenly charred, about 10 minutes. Serve with honey mustard.

SERVES 4

EGGPLANT CURRY

This delectable curry takes no time to prepare. Serve with rice and a sweet chutney.

6 tablespoons vegetable oil
1 large eggplant, unpeeled and cubed
salt
1 onion, diced
1 tablespoon minced garlic
1 tablespoon minced fresh ginger
1 tablespoon curry powder
$\frac{1}{2}$ teaspoon ground cumin
$\frac{1}{4}$ teaspoon cinnamon
$\frac{1}{8}$ teaspoon turmeric
$\frac{1}{4}$ teaspoon cayenne
2 tablespoons tomato paste
1 cup water
$1\frac{1}{2}$ tablespoons sugar
1 bunch spinach, washed and roughly
    chopped
1 tomato, chopped

Heat 4 tablespoons of the oil in a large heavy pot over high heat. Sauté eggplant with salt until soft and golden. Drain on paper towels.

Add remaining 2 tablespoons oil to pot and reduce heat to medium. Sauté onion, garlic, and ginger until soft. Add curry powder, cumin, cinnamon, turmeric, cayenne, and tomato paste, and cook, stirring constantly, about 1 minute.

Add water and sugar, bring to a boil, and cook 1 minute longer at high heat. Stir in spinach and cook until wilted. Add eggplant and tomato, reduce heat, and cook just to blend flavors, about 4 minutes. Adjust seasonings and serve hot over rice.

SERVES 4

EGGPLANT TOMATO LASAGNE

In this buffet favorite, eggplant slices are roasted rather than fried, for a minimum of fat.

2 medium eggplants, unpeeled
    and cut crosswise in $1/4$-inch slices
olive oil
salt
$3/4$ pound lasagne noodles or 3 sheets
    fresh egg pasta
double the recipe for "Tomato Sauce"
    (see page 50)
1 pound fresh mozzarella cheese,
    chopped, or grated if not fresh
1 cup grated Parmesan cheese

Preheat oven to 450 degrees F.
Arrange eggplant slices in single layer

on oil-coated sheets. Drizzle with oil, season with salt, and roast about 10 minutes per side. Reduce heat to 350 degrees F.

If using dry noodles, boil, drain, and rinse with cold water. Reserve in a bowl of iced water. Fresh pasta need not be cooked, simply trim to fit pan.

Coat 9 x 13-inch lasagne pan with tomato sauce. Cover with single layer of pasta and top with half the eggplant. Spoon one-third of the tomato sauce on top and cover with half the mozzarella. Repeat layers, ending with a layer of pasta topped by tomato sauce. Sprinkle with Parmesan and bake 45 minutes, until golden and bubbly. Cool slightly before serving.

SERVES 6 TO 8

EGGPLANT AND SUN-DRIED TOMATO FRITTATA

Open-face Italian omelets are excellent for entertaining since they are delicious at room temperature.

5 tablespoons olive oil
1 small eggplant, unpeeled and diced
5 large eggs
$1/4$ cup grated Parmesan cheese
2 tablespoons minced sun-dried tomatoes in oil
2 to 3 dashes Tabasco
freshly ground black pepper
1 tablespoon butter

Heat 4 tablespoons of the oil in large skillet over high heat. Sauté eggplant until evenly browned, about 5 minutes. Drain on paper towels.

In bowl, whisk together eggs, Parmesan, sun-dried tomatoes, Tabasco, and black pepper. Gently stir in eggplant.

Preheat broiler and move rack 6 inches from flame.

Heat butter and remaining tablespoon of oil in medium ovenproof skillet over high heat. Pour in egg mixture, swirl to coat pan, and cook to set bottom, less than 1 minute. Reduce heat to low and cook until sides are set and center is runny. Transfer to broiler just to set top, less than 1 minute. Cool in pan 5 minutes, then transfer to platter and cut in wedges to serve.

SERVES 6

LIGHTENED MOUSSAKA

The traditional white sauce has been replaced with just a thin layer of melted cheese in this updated Greek classic.

2 tablespoons olive oil
1 onion, diced
1½ tablespoons minced garlic
2 pounds ground lamb
salt and freshly ground pepper
½ teaspoon allspice
¼ teaspoon ground nutmeg
1 cup dry white wine
2 cups canned tomatoes, drained
　　and chopped
1 tablespoon dried crumbled oregano
2 large eggplants, peeled and thinly
　　sliced lengthwise
1 cup grated mozzarella cheese
½ cup grated Parmesan cheese

Heat 2 tablespoons oil in Dutch oven over moderate heat. Sauté onion and garlic until soft. Add lamb, salt, pepper, allspice, and nutmeg. Turn up heat and cook until browned. Pour in wine and boil 5 minutes. Stir in tomatoes and oregano, reduce heat, and cook, uncovered, until nearly dry.

Roast eggplant slices in single layer on oiled pans in 450 degrees F oven, about 10 minutes per side. Reduce heat to 350 degrees F.

Oil 9 x 13-inch lasagne pan. Line bottom with half of the eggplant slices. Add meat in even layer. Top with remaining eggplant and sprinkle with cheeses. Cover with foil and bake 40 minutes, until casserole is bubbly. Let cool, cut, and serve.

SERVES 6 TO 8

Turkish Delight

It was the Ottoman Turks in the 16th century who first recognized eggplant's culinary possibilities. They dubbed it "lord of vegetables" or sayyid al-khudar, *and Turkish chefs are said to have one hundred methods for preparing it. The Turks spread their passion into the Balkans, Russia, and throughout the Middle East, where it eventually spread to North Africa, and then Europe via Spain. According to food historian Charles Perry, one city, Denizli, in western Turkey claims no fewer than thirty traditional eggplant dishes.*

SUCCULENT
SALADS AND
SANDWICHES

ORZO WITH EGGPLANT AND PEPPERS

Eggplant has the character to hold its own in the company of strong flavors like feta cheese and raisins.

³/₄ cup olive oil
¹/₂ teaspoon red chile flakes
2 tablespoons minced garlic
3 tablespoons red wine vinegar
¹/₄ cup chopped fresh mint
1 pound orzo, riso, *or* other small pasta, cooked, drained, and rinsed with cold water
1 red bell pepper, roasted, peeled, seeded, and diced
²/₃ cup crumbled feta cheese
¹/₂ cup raisins
1 medium eggplant, trimmed and diced
salt and freshly ground black pepper

Combine ½ cup of the olive oil in small pan with chile flakes and garlic. Cook over moderate heat, swirling occasionally, until garlic is soft and oil is infused. Let cool. When room temperature, transfer to small bowl and whisk in vinegar and mint. Pour over cooked pasta in large bowl, and mix to coat evenly.

Add red bell pepper, feta, and raisins. Stir to combine.

Heat remaining ¼ cup oil in nonstick pan over high heat. Sauté eggplant until evenly browned, about 3 minutes. Cool slightly, then add to salad. Season to taste with salt and pepper, gently toss, and serve room temperature or chilled.

SERVES 4 TO 8

COUSCOUS WITH EGGPLANT AND PINE NUTS

This cold grain salad is substantial enough to serve as a main course.

1 cup water
6 tablespoons olive oil
3 tablespoons lemon juice
1 teaspoon ground cumin
$\frac{1}{4}$ teaspoon ground cinnamon
salt and freshly ground pepper
1 cup instant couscous
1 medium eggplant, unpeeled and
  diced
$\frac{1}{4}$ cup pine nuts, toasted
$\frac{1}{4}$ cup chopped fresh Italian parsley
$\frac{1}{2}$ medium onion, diced

Combine water, 2 tablespoons each of olive oil and lemon juice, cumin, cinnamon, salt, and pepper in medium saucepan. Bring to boil. Stir in couscous, cover, and remove from heat. Let sit 15 minutes.

Meanwhile heat remaining olive oil in large skillet over high heat and sauté eggplant until evenly browned, about 5 minutes. Drain on paper towels.

Transfer couscous to large bowl and toss with fork to separate. Add pine nuts, parsley, onion, and eggplant, and gently mix to combine. Sprinkle with remaining lemon juice, and serve or chill.

SERVES 4 TO 6

SICILIAN ROASTED VEGETABLE SALAD

The idea for this stylish salad came from my local trattoria, where it is called "contadina," or peasant salad.

2 Japanese eggplants, trimmed and
    thinly sliced diagonally
1 zucchini, thinly sliced diagonally
olive oil for brushing
salt
2 cups mixed salad greens
4 ounces soft goat cheese
1 roasted red pepper, peeled,
    seeded, and cut into 6 slices
freshly ground pepper
1 tablespoon balsamic vinegar
2 tablespoons olive oil

Preheat broiler and arrange rack 8 inches from heat. Coat tray with olive oil and arrange eggplant and zucchini slices in single layer. Sprinkle with salt, and broil until lightly and evenly charred, turning frequently.

Line serving platter with salad greens and stack goat cheese in center in two portions. Arrange red pepper strips in spoke pattern, followed by a circle of eggplant and zucchini. Season vegetables with salt and pepper, and cheese with pepper. Whisk together vinegar and oil and drizzle over all.

SERVES 2

SEARED TUNA AND EGGPLANT

For a special presentation, garnish this elegant salad with boiled potatoes cut in wedges, cherry tomatoes, and blanched green beans.

2 medium eggplants, trimmed, peeled, and cut crosswise into $\frac{1}{4}$-inch slices
olive oil
salt
6 cups mixed salad greens, washed and torn
12 green garlic olives
4 eggs, hard-boiled, peeled, and halved
$\frac{1}{2}$ cup plus 2 tablespoons olive oil
$\frac{1}{4}$ cup lemon juice
freshly ground pepper
4 (4-ounce) tuna fillets

Preheat oven to 450 degrees F. Lightly coat baking tray with olive oil and arrange eggplant in single layer. Sprinkle with oil and salt, and roast about 10 minutes per side, until charred.

On 4 serving plates arrange a bed of lettuce on one side and a layer of eggplant slices on the other. Top the salad with 4 olives each and place an egg half on either side.

In small bowl whisk together 1/2 cup olive oil, lemon juice, salt, and pepper. Spoon over greens, eggs, and eggplant.

Heat remaining oil in large skillet over high heat. Season tuna all over with salt and pepper. Sauté about 3 minutes per side. Place each in center of plate, garnish with remaining dressing, and serve.

SERVES 4

GRILLED CHICKEN BABA GHANOUSH SANDWICH

Thinly sliced leg of lamb can be substituted for chicken in this lusty Mediterranean sandwich.

4 skinless, boneless chicken
  breast halves, pounded
salt and freshly ground pepper
1/4 cup olive oil
2 teaspoons minced garlic
1 tablespoon *herbes de Provence*
4 pita breads, warmed
1 1/2 cups "Baba Ghanoush" (see
  recipe, page 18)
2 tomatoes, thinly sliced

Preheat grill of broiler.
Season chicken all over with
salt and pepper. In small bowl,
whisk together olive oil, garlic,
and herbs. Brush mixture all over
chicken breasts.

Grill or broil chicken about 6 minutes per side. Cut into thin strips. Cut
pitas in half and generously spread one
side with baba ghanoush. Place tomato
slices on top and fill with chicken strips.

SERVES 4

To Salt or Not to Salt
Cooks sprinkle salt on eggplant to eliminate
excess moisture, thereby reducing bitterness and
oil absorption. The salting step (it takes about
30 minutes) may always be eliminated—it
really is a matter of preference. I notice very
little difference in taste between salted and
unsalted eggplant.

GRILLED EGGPLANT AND ARUGULA SANDWICH

Peppery greens and thinly sliced onion cut the unctuousness of eggplant without masking its flavor. A simple favorite for the eggplant obsessed.

$1/2$ cup olive oil
2 teaspoons minced garlic
1 teaspoon herbes de Provence
salt and freshly ground pepper
1 large Japanese eggplant,
   trimmed and thinly sliced
   lengthwise
2 thick slices rustic country bread
thinly sliced onion
6 leaves arugula

Preheat broiler. Whisk together olive oil, garlic, herbs, salt, and pepper. Brush all over eggplant slices and bread and arrange on baking tray.

Grill eggplant and bread until lightly charred on both sides. Make sandwich by placing eggplant slices on one bread slice. Top with a few onion slices, arugula, and bread. Slice and serve.

MAKES 1

When eggplant was first introduced to Italy in the 15th century, it was considered a dangerous substance. People fed them to their goats before eating them themselves—perhaps explaining the Italian word for eggplant, melanzana. *Modern Sicilians are masters of eggplant cookery and many American favorites, such as eggplant parmesan, originated there.*

The French Way with Eggplant
*French cooks reluctantly took to
eggplant, or aubergine as they called
it, late in the 18th century after it
was introduced by Louis XIV. It was
used externally for hemorrhoids,
burns, and inflammations before it
found its way into the frying pan and
into such classic dishes as rata-
touille. It is integral to Southern
France's peasant cooking, and for
that reason was traditionally considered beneath the elevated palates of
haughty northerners.*

SUPPORTING PLAYERS

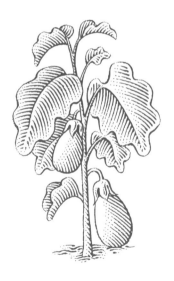

ROASTED EGGPLANT, POTATOES, AND PEPPERS

Friend and food lover Michael Villella came up with this roasted alternative to caponata. It tastes great with any grilled or roasted meat and makes an excellent light meal.

olive oil for coating
1 large eggplant, peeled and cut into
   1-inch cubes
1 baking potato, unpeeled and cut into
   1/2-inch cubes
1 cup coarsely chopped onion
1 red bell pepper, roasted, seeded, peeled,
   and cut into 1/2-inch squares
3 garlic cloves, chopped
1/2 cup olive oil
2 1/2 teaspoons dried crushed oregano
1 teaspoon coarse salt
freshly ground pepper

Preheat oven to 475 degrees F. Lightly coat 9 x 12-inch roasting pan with olive oil.

Combine eggplant, potato, onion, red pepper, and garlic in large mixing bowl. Stir to combine. Add olive oil, salt, and pepper, and toss again to evenly coat. Spread mixture in prepared pan and bake about 40 minutes, until vegetables soften and edges of eggplant begin to caramelize. Serve at room temperature.

SERVES 4

Peeling eggplant represents a trade-off. The skin adds a beautiful deep purple color, but it also has an unfortunate tendency to stick between teeth and cause indigestion in unlucky eaters.

RATATOUILLE

Here's the classic Provençal vegetable stew and condiment.

1/2 cup olive oil

2 onions, chopped

8 garlic cloves, minced

salt and freshly ground pepper

1/4 teaspoon dried red chile flakes

2 red bell peppers, cored, seeded, and cut into 1-inch squares

4 Japanese eggplants, trimmed and cut into 1/2-inch dice

3 medium zucchinis, trimmed and cut into 1/2-inch dice

1/4 pound French green beans, trimmed and cut in 1/2-inch lengths

1 (28-ounce) can Italian peeled tomatoes, drained and chopped

3 tablespoons chopped fresh basil, thyme, tarragon and/or rosemary or 1 tablespoon dried

2 tablespoons lemon juice

Heat $\frac{1}{4}$ cup of the olive oil in large heavy pot over medium heat. Sauté onions and garlic with salt, pepper, and chile flakes until onions soften. Add red bell pepper and cook, stirring frequently, another 10 minutes.

Add eggplants, zucchinis, French beans, remaining olive oil, tomatoes, and herbs. Bring to boil, reduce to simmer, and cook, covered, until vegetables are soft and flavors blend, about 40 minutes. Stir in lemon juice and remove from heat. Adjust seasonings with salt and pepper, and serve hot, chilled, or room temperature.

SERVES 6 TO 8

RICE EGGPLANT PANCAKES

These savory pancakes can be topped with a dollop of plain yogurt and some diced tomatoes for a more elegant presentation.

2 cups cold cooked rice
6 Japanese eggplants, peeled and
   finely grated
2 eggs, beaten
1 teaspoon garlic powder
$\frac{1}{2}$ teaspoon ground cumin
$\frac{1}{2}$ teaspoon salt
freshly ground pepper
olive oil for frying

Combine rice, eggplant, eggs, garlic powder, cumin, salt, and pepper in medium mixing bowl.

Pour oil into large frying pan to a depth of ¼ inch. Place over medium-high heat. Spoon generous tablespoonfuls of batter into hot oil, and press to flatten with spatula. Fry until golden brown on both sides. Transfer to paper towels to drain and serve hot.

SERVES 4, MAKES 12

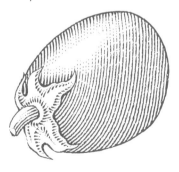

ROASTED GARLIC EGGPLANT FLANS

Serve these plain-looking but delicious custards with an elegant leg of lamb or roast beef. Add color by garnishing with roasted red pepper strips or diced tomatoes.

1 head garlic, top trimmed
1 large eggplant, stemmed and
　halved lengthwise
olive oil for sprinkling
salt
$\frac{1}{2}$ cup heavy cream
2 eggs
freshly ground pepper
butter *or* nonstick spray
　for coating

Preheat oven to 425 degrees F. Place garlic head and eggplant halves on baking tray. Score eggplant, drizzle oil over all, and sprinkle with salt. Roast until soft: 30 minutes for garlic and 50 to 60 minutes for eggplant. Reduce oven to 325 degrees F. Let vegetables cool, scrape out eggplant pulp, and press garlic cloves to peel.

In food processor with metal blade, combine eggplant, garlic, cream, eggs, pepper, and salt. Purée until smooth.

Coat 4 half cup (4-ounce) ramekins with butter or spray. Fill with purée and transfer cups to larger roasting pan. Fill with hot water halfway up sides of ramekins. Bake until the tip of a knife inserted in the center comes out clean, about 1 hour. Remove to cool and invert to serve.

MAKES 4

GRILLED EGGPLANT MISO

Miso, available in health food stores and Asian markets, is a high-protein seasoning paste of fermented soybeans.

4 Japanese eggplants, trimmed
  and quartered lengthwise
peanut oil
salt
$1/3$ cup rice vinegar
1 tablespoon miso
2 teaspoons minced fresh ginger
1 teaspoon minced garlic
$1/4$ teaspoon red chile flakes
$1/3$ cup peanut oil

Preheat grill or broiler.
Lightly coat eggplants with
peanut oil and grill until
browned, about 2 minutes per
side. Transfer to serving platter or
shallow bowl and sprinkle with salt.

Whisk together remaining ingredients and pour over eggplant. Toss to
coat evenly. Serve room temperature
or chill.

SERVES 4

Botanical Roots
Eggplant is a member of the family of plants
classified as nightshade. Technically it is a fruit,
but for legal, cooking, and eating purposes it is
a vegetable. Other members are pepper, tomato,
tobacco, the hallucinogenic jimsonweed, and
poisonous nightshade. The botanical name is
Solanum melongena.

GARLIC-MARINATED EGGPLANT

These garlicky tidbits are handy for summer buffets and picnics.

4 Japanese eggplants, unpeeled, trimmed, and quartered lengthwise
olive oil
salt
2½ tablespoons olive oil
1 tablespoon plus 1 teaspoon lemon juice
1 tablespoon plus 1 teaspoon red wine vinegar
2 teaspoons minced garlic
½ teaspoon red chile flakes
2 tablespoons chopped fresh mint

Preheat oven to 450 degrees F. Arrange eggplant on oil-coated baking tray, sprinkle with olive oil and salt, and roast until soft and slightly charred, about 20 minutes.

In ceramic or glass casserole, whisk together remaining ingredients with salt to taste. Add eggplant and toss to marinate evenly. Cover with plastic and chill up to 3 days.

SERVES 4 TO 6

The Eggplant Diet
Eggplant plays a major role in the diet of most vegetarian cultures. Because it provides the bulk and texture that is sometimes missing in a meatless diet, it is often used as a meat substitute. As an added bonus, it is extremely low in calories. One cup contains only about 30 calories.
It is also an excellent source of folic acid, potassium, and fiber.

SZECHUAN EGGPLANT

If you like your eggplant hot and spicy, here is the dish.

1 tablespoon ground bean paste
  or hoisin sauce
2 tablespoons soy sauce
2 tablespoons dry sherry
2 tablespoons balsamic vinegar
2 tablespoons sugar
$1/2$ teaspoon Chinese chile oil
$1/4$ teaspoon red chile flakes
$1/4$ cup peanut oil
$1/4$ cup minced garlic
1 tablespoon minced fresh ginger
$1^1/2$ pounds Japanese eggplant,
  trimmed and thinly sliced
  diagonally

In small bowl, combine bean paste or hoisin, soy sauce, sherry, vinegar, sugar, chile oil, and red chile flakes.

Heat peanut oil in large skillet or wok over high heat. Stir-fry garlic and ginger less than 1 minute. Add eggplant and fry until lightly golden, about 5 minutes. Pour in sauce mixture, toss to coat evenly, cover, and reduce heat to low. Cook about 5 minutes longer, remove cover, and continue to cook until sauce is thickened to taste. Serve hot.

SERVES 6

Eggplant's Best Seasonings
Oregano, basil, and mint are always delicious with eggplant. The vegetables that grow alongside it in the garden are also its natural companions: Tomatoes, bell peppers, and zucchini, combined with garlic and olive oil (with a touch of salt) are always unbeatable.

BABY EGGPLANTS WITH OLIVES AND PINE NUTS

This elegant dish can also be served as a light entreé.

4 Japanese eggplants, trimmed
olive oil for coating
salt
2 tablespoons olive oil
2 teaspoons minced garlic
$1/2$ cup plain bread crumbs
$1/4$ cup pine nuts, roughly chopped
$3/4$ cup Kalamata olives, pitted and
    chopped
1 tablespoon chopped fresh mint
1 egg, beaten
freshly ground pepper

Preheat oven to 400 degrees F.

Cut eggplants in half lengthwise and lightly score. Lightly oil all over, sprinkle tops with salt and bake, cut-side up,

25 to 30 minutes, until soft. Let cool. When cool enough to handle, scrape out pulp and chop, reserving shells. Reduce oven to 350 degrees F.

Heat the olive oil in small skillet over high heat. Add chopped eggplant and garlic, and sauté until nearly dry. Transfer to mixing bowl.

In another bowl, combine bread crumbs and pine nuts.

Add $\frac{1}{4}$ cup pine nut mixture to chopped eggplant, along with olives, mint, egg, and pepper to taste. Mix well.

Lightly coat ovenproof casserole with olive oil. Arrange eggplant shells, cut-side up, and stuff with olive mixture, tamping down to fill. Sprinkle tops with remaining bread crumb mixture, sprinkle generously with olive oil, and bake about 20 minutes, until tops are golden. Serve hot.

SERVES 4

EGGPLANT
RICOTTA ROLLS

1 large eggplant, unpeeled and cut
   into ½-inch slices lengthwise
salt
2 eggs
¾ cup bread crumbs
1¼ cups grated Parmesan cheese
¾ cup olive oil
1 cup ricotta cheese
¼ teaspoon ground nutmeg
freshly ground pepper
1 cup tomato sauce

Sprinkle eggplant slices with salt
and arrange in colander to drain 30
minutes. Pat dry with paper towels.

Beat eggs in a shallow dish and
combine the bread crumbs and ½
cup of the Parmesan in another dish
for dipping. Dip each slice first in
eggs and then in bread crumb mixture to coat, shaking off excess.

Heat oil in large skillet over high heat. Fry slices in single layer, being careful not to crowd the pan, until golden on both sides. Transfer to paper towels to drain, and blot excess oil. Meanwhile preheat oven to 350 degrees F.

Mix ricotta, $1/2$ cup of Parmesan, and nutmeg in bowl. Season with salt and pepper.

Spoon $1/4$ cup tomato sauce on bottom of 9-inch-square ovenproof casserole. When eggplant is cool enough to handle, place about $1^1/2$ tablespoons of cheese mixture in center of each slice and fold over, across width, to enclose. Arrange in baking dish, seam-side down, so rolls slightly overlap. Coat with remaining tomato sauce, sprinkle with remaining Parmesan, and cover with foil. Bake until cheese melts and sauce is bubbly, about 40 minutes. Serve hot.

SERVES 4

CONVERSIONS

LIQUID
1 Tbsp = 15 ml
$^1/_2$ cup = 4 fl oz = 125 ml
1 cup = 8 fl oz = 250 ml

DRY
$^1/_4$ cup = 4 Tbsp = 2 oz = 60 g
1 cup = $^1/_2$ pound = 8 oz = 250 g

FLOUR
$^1/_2$ cup = 60 g
1 cup = 4 oz = 125 g

TEMPERATURE
400° F = 200° C = gas mark 6
375° F = 190° C = gas mark 5
350° F = 175° C = gas mark 4

MISCELLANEOUS
2 Tbsp butter = 1 oz = 30 g
1 inch = 2.5 cm
all-purpose flour = plain flour
baking soda = bicarbonate of soda
brown sugar = demerara sugar
confectioners' sugar = icing sugar
heavy cream = double cream
molasses = black treacle
raisins = sultanas
rolled oats = oat flakes
semisweet chocolate = plain chocolate
sugar = caster sugar